Lenore
Finds a Friend

A True Story from Bedlam Farm

Story and photographs by

Jon Katz

Henry Holt and Company

NEW YORK

Henry Holt and Company, LLC
Publishers since 1866
175 Fifth Avenue
New York, New York 10010
mackids.com

Henry Holt® is a registered trademark
of Henry Holt and Company, LLC.

Library of Congress Cataloging-in-
Publication Data
Katz, Jon.
Lenore finds a friend : a true story
from Bedlam Farm / Story and photographs
by Jon Katz. — 1st ed.
p.   cm.
ISBN 978-0-8050-9220-2 (hc)
1. Working dogs—New York (State)—
Anecdotes—Juvenile literature. 2. Farm
life—New York (State)—West Hebron—
Anecdotes—Juvenile literature.
3. Social behavior in animals—Anecdotes—
Juvenile literature. 4. Animals—Anecdotes.
5. Emotions in animals—Anecdotes—Juvenile
literature. 6. Animal communication—
Juvenile literature. 7. Bedlam Farm (West
Hebron, N.Y.)—Juvenile literature. I. Title.
SF428.2.K378 2012   636.7309747'1—dc23
2011029040

First Edition—2012 / Designed by April Ward
Printed in China by Macmillan Production
Asia Ltd., Kwun Tong, Kowloon, Hong Kong
(vendor code: 10)

10 9 8 7 6 5 4 3 2 1

*For
Lenore, Frieda,
Izzy, and Rose*

When Lenore came
to Bedlam Farm,
she was just a puppy.

None of the other animals
wanted to be her friend.

Even when Lenore got older,
the other animals
were not friendly.
The rooster crowed at her.

The donkey tried to kick her.

The goats just jeered.

The dog named Rose
was too busy
to be Lenore's friend.

Rose had a job.

She took care of the sheep.

She kept them safe
while they ate grass on the hills
around the farm.

Once, Lenore tried
to lick Rose on the nose.
Rose didn't like it.
She had no time
for Lenore.

Lenore ran off
and hid in the grass.

Suddenly, she looked up.

A grumpy ram named Brutus
was standing right in front of her!

Lenore gave Brutus a big kiss on his nose.

Brutus had never been kissed before.

He turned away.

Lenore walked slowly
back to the farmhouse.
She felt sad.

The next day,

Lenore waited for Brutus.

She kissed him on the nose again!

At first, Brutus looked as if
he wanted to kick Lenore.
No one had ever tried
to be his friend before.

Lenore wagged her tail.
Brutus put his head down
near the ground.

Lenore kissed Brutus
on the nose again.

Then she rolled over
to show she wanted to play.

Soon, Rose came charging over.
She barked and nipped
at Brutus's legs
to make him go back
to the rest of the sheep,
where he belonged.
She growled at Lenore.

Lenore went slowly
back to the farmhouse.
She felt sad again.

But Lenore was not about
to give up on the first friend
she had ever made.

The next morning,
Lenore followed Rose and the sheep
to the pasture.

She wanted to find Brutus again.

Brutus was happy
to see his new friend.
He put his head down
so they could touch noses.

Soon, Lenore was happily eating grass

alongside Brutus—

and grass is not what dogs usually eat.

Rose came running up
to move the flock
and chase Lenore away.

But this time,
Lenore wouldn't move
and neither would Brutus.

Rose was puzzled.

Why would a dog

want to be friends with a ram?

27

Rose watched them for a while,
then nodded once
and looked away.

She never bothered

Lenore and Brutus again.

Lenore finally had a friend.

This gave her a new idea.

The next day, Lenore brought Rose
a toy and a biscuit.
Then she kissed her on the nose.

Now Rose has a friend, too.

Author's Note

This is a true story.

Rose is a border collie, a working dog who takes care of the sheep and helps run Bedlam Farm.

Brutus is an eight-year-old ram who now lives on a sheep farm in Vermont with his sons and daughters.

Lenore has very loving ways and makes everyone smile. She has a lot of friends now on Bedlam Farm.